# HOW TO MAKE MONEY ONLINE

HOW TO EARN MONEY ONLINE POST CORONA

MAHI TANEJA

**Xpress**Publishing
An imprint of Notion Press

No.8, 3rd Cross Street,CIT Colony,
Mylapore, Chennai, Tamil Nadu-600004

ISBN 978-1-63669-835-9

# Contents

# Preface

*This book contains researched information to make money online . Some methods are tried and tested on my own . I'll discuss some popular and unpopular methods to earn online in this book with changing time post corona effect . I'll also mention some sectors where you can earn as a side business with minimum effort and investment. I hope you ll be able to make a wealthy lifestyle and get some new ideas to earn money.*

# Acknowledgements

*This book is cowriten by parth taneja who has writen many books on meditation and general life problems he is also an expert on online money making businesses.*

*For meditation and spiritualism books you can buy .*

*How to live a happy life by parth taneja*

*How to stop overthinking by parth taneja*

*Budhha life and few stories by parth taneja*

*discover yourself ; the young meditator by parth taneja*

# CHAPTER ONE

# SOCIAL MEDIA INFLUENCERS

*The new trend and most common method to earn online is turning out to be an social media influencer . In this online business module you have to create a content which is most trending and find audience to build an online page . Once you reach a few thousand followers you can start earning . There are a lot of methods to earn online .*

*Most common method is to give shoutout to other small influencers and they ll pay you to advitise their account via your stories or posts. The other way to earn via this social media account is to sell self products of other products on the page .*

*Best way to earn through this page is turning out to be an Amazon influencer , being an amazon influencer you will get your own page and cam easily sell products listed on Amazon.*

*If anybody clicks on the link you posted on your page and do not buy anything from that page of amazon but buys something else within two days from Amazon you ll receive some comission via Amazon for that sale and that can be a lot if your page size above 50k .*

# CHAPTER TWO

# DROP SHIPPING BUSINESS

*What if i say there is an online business where you don't need to invest much but you can get returns in millions . Yes it's true if you start a drop shipping business . In a drop shipping business you have to make your own store on any platform you like .*

*This business works as you ll select some products from various sites like alibaba most commonly used for it and will list them on your ebay/Shopify store or any other platform you like .*

*A question might come to your mind if i have to sell products how would it be in less investment . Well here is how you ll select any product from a big site like alibaba and list it with higher price on your site.*

*This project is to be market by yourself and little investment. You dont need to buy the product unless any order comes to you . If an order comes you ll buy the product from that site and it will delver directly to the person who gave you order and you ll make money being a middle man.*

# CHAPTER THREE

# BLOGGING

*Being a blogger is completely different than being a writer you can write blogs about anything you want small topics . You can select a specific niche to blog or be a free blogger .*

*Starting to engage audience might be bit difficult to engage audience. You ll need to add your friends and close ones to your blog so it can be shared initially . There is a platform by Microsoft by the name blogger . com which allows you to create a free account.*

*How do we earn blogging? Its pretty simple you can run google advertisement on your blog so google will start showing adds on your page and you ll get some some money monthly via google. You can tie up with companies of your field and ask them to pay you money for mentioning their products in your blogs . This method is pretty easy to follow and you must try it for once .*

# CHAPTER FOUR

# FREELANCING

*If you possess any useful skill other might need but not have freelance is the business for you . You can help in hundreds of ways to get money from free lancing. Being a freelancer you have to do a work for someone who need it to be done .*

*When that work is done you dilver it to the person through the site you got work on first place and wether he likes your work or not he will have to pay for the work you have done .*

*What kind of work has to be done in freelance ? There are a numerous work to be done in freelance you can create presentation online for people , market their products, design logos ,design book cover, business cards , marketing skills , edit books , translate languages , write on recent topics and many more. Leading freelancing platforms are fiver and freelancer .com . Its easy to register and bid on various works .*

# CHAPTER FIVE

# YOUTUBER

*Being youtuber is most common trend among present generation to earn online when you become a you tuber you have to post videos on you tube platform the interface of you tube is very simple and millions of people are earing a quite some of money via you tube videos.*

*You tube turn on ads on your videos and give you part of the money your video generates . Almost everyone is aware of how you tube works so i wont go in deeper layers of this topic for any questions regarding you tube you can contact me on instagram or email me .*

# CHAPTER SIX

# Drop Servicing

*Just like drop shipping you can try out drop service business the difference between drop service and shipping is that you provide services instead of products . In recent times drop shipping business is becoming crowded so drop shipping is the next drop for this business*

*How to drop service? For drop services you would have to make a website for the service you are thinking to drop . For example if you want to provide logos for companies you ll create a website on google This site needs to look like a professional website you ll mention your service for much higher rates you are getting it from fiver or freelancer .*

*What will you do when an order comes is that website is simple you ll pass the order to any freelancer easily available of fiver at much cheaper rates and dilver the service asked . You would have to invest some money in marketing of the website. But returns can be 10 times more than your investment.*

# CHAPTER SEVEN

# RESELLING

*There are some websites that allow you to resell their products to your closer circle . It works like this it creates a small website for you and you can add your products from the website to the page and the person will never know where the product is coming from , the bill will show your name on the product .*

*These applications are just a startup focused in india i am not sure for other countries leading companies in india to resell the products are meesho and grow.*

# CHAPTER EIGHT

# LIVE STREAMING ONLINE GAMES

*One of most popular way to earn through gaming is now to stream your live game on platforms like you tube and then collect money directly from viewers giving shout-out and selling memberships to viewers.*

*You can also participate in various competitions online about that particular game and win prize amount .*

# CHAPTER NINE

# Selling on etsy

*If you are in creative field and make handmade stuff , jewel , cosmetic, dresses or anything similar you can use etsy as a platform to sell your products it has been considered to be the best platform for any handmade products.*

*Registration on etsy is quite simple you can ship your products world wide using etsy and reach targeted audience . In better ways.*

# CHAPTER TEN

# STOCK MARKET

*Moving on from earning that you made from these methods or any job you do how can you make money from existing money you have without doing much work ?*

*Share market is the answer for you , there are hundreds and thousands of companies listed in share markets of each and every country that can help you to grow money exponentially*

*How does share market work ?*

*Companies you might have heard names of offers some percentage of company to general public in form of shares . These shares can be brought at a market price and the price of share is affected by the company's overall turnover and market value .*

*The more you can hold a share there is more possibility that you can sell the share at a higher price but it can be risky sometimes as share price might go down to nothing but that doesn't happen in general cases .*

# CHAPTER ELEVEN

# IPO (Initial public offering)

*What is ipo ?*

*When a company is listed for the first time in share market it is known as in ipo . Ipo is the fund needed by company from general public and in return they give you their company shares as holdings .*

*How can this help us to make money ?*

*These ipo are generally sold at a very lower price than their actual value as soon as IPOs come in market the share value of that particular stock doubles or triples in a very short period of some in many cases.*

*You can message my coauthor parth to tell you which application india can you use to apply for an ipo.*

# CHAPTER TWELVE

# MUTUAL FUNDS

*Moving on from risky share market you can also make money in mutual funds . To understand the difference between a share market and a mutual fund i would like to share and example.*

*Suppose you want to invest 1000$ in share market , the companys that you want yo invest in have a share price of 1500$ or more and there are 10-20 such compaines you want to invest in how can you invest in all of them with such low budget.*

*Now what does a mutual fund do is to create a fund of large investment in these companies they buy lot if share in a lot of companies and make a separate share for the fund which is very very low as compared to the company's share they are holding .*

*For example a mutual fund is holding its shares in all those companies you wanted to invest in but those companies share price were very high but this mutual fund who is holding exactly same compaies has a share price of 100$ per share .*

*In this manner it lowers the risk of loss as even if a company goes down in 20 compaines your share price wont be much affected and you can purchase shares of earlier companies indirectly at a very low price .*

*As in my example now you can buy 10 shares of 100 dollar each and your investment is well distributed in the market and will not go down easily as it would have been in direct stock investment*

# SELLING ON ECOMMERCE

*Easiest way to get your reach to millions of coustmers is to sell on ECOMMERCE website such as amazon so that your product is available to more and more consumers possible.*

*Platform such as ebay can also be an good alternative to sell used products and modified ones.*

# WRITING A BOOK

*If you are reading a book there is a huge possibility that you have given money to amazon to read it if so i must be receiving some royalty out of it . Yes writing and publishing a book isn't much difficult as you might to think it is so .*

*I would recommend to get some interesting topic and start writing your own books.*

# About Author

*I am young entrepreneur/writer/meditator/investor at just 19 years of age i have tried almost everything i wrote in this book gained experience in various fields and now am sharing my research and experience with everyone in the world so that they can invest/earn well in this volatile market . I hope you have liked this book if so then please let me know.*

*You can message my co author at*

*instagram _taneja.parth_*

*Or email him at tanejaparth246@gmail.com*

www.ingramcontent.com/pod-product-compliance
Lightning Source LLC
Chambersburg PA
CBHW061522180526
45171CB00001B/299